FOREST BOOKS

FISH-RINGS ON WATER

KATHERINE GALLAGHER was born in Maldon, Victoria, Australia in September 1935, and grew up on a 700-acre sheep and wheat farm near Bendigo, Victoria. She has a B.A. and a Diploma of Education from Melbourne University. She started writing poetry in 1965. After some years teaching, she travelled to Europe in 1969, living first in London and then in Paris where she wrote her first book, *The Eye's Circle*, published in 1975 by Rigmarole Books, Melbourne. In 1978, *Tributaries of the Love-Song* (Angus & Robertson, Sydney) appeared. Her work has been published widely in Australia and the U.K. In 1981, she won the Brisbane Warana Award. Her third widely-acclaimed collection, *Passengers to the City*, published in 1985 by Hale & Iremonger, Sydney, was shortlisted for the 1986 Australian National Poetry Award. She is also a short-story writer and currently lives in London with her husband and son.

PIERRE VELLA was born in 1938 in Paris where he still lives. He has published three collections of poetry and illustrated many books. A painter, engraver and sculptor, he has had numerous exhibitions in France and abroad.

Katherine Gallagher

FISH-RINGS
ON
WATER

POEMS
by
KATHERINE GALLAGHER

Introduced
by
PETER PORTER

For Dear Katie,
jet-setting beaver of the maple
leaf and scribe extraordinaire
with lots of love and a hug,
Katherine
London '89.
Vive la poésie!

FOREST BOOKS
LONDON ☆ 1989 ☆ BOSTON

PUBLISHED BY
FOREST BOOKS

20 Forest View, Chingford, London E4 7AY, U.K.
P.O. Box 438, Wayland, MA 01778, U.S.A.

First published 1989

Typeset in Great Britain by Cover to Cover, Cambridge
Printed in Great Britain by BPCC Wheatons Ltd, Exeter

British Library Cataloguing in Publication Data
Gallagher, Katherine, 1935—
Fish-rings on water: poems
I. Title
821

ISBN 0–948259–75–2

Library of Congress Catalogue Card No
89–85182

For Bernard and Julien
and to the memory of my Mother

Acknowledgements

Acknowledgements are due to the following where some of these poems first appeared: *B.B.C. GCSE Poetry Booklet, Distaff, Feminist Review, Foolscap, Footnotes, Jennings, Other Poetry, Outposts, Resurgence, The Bound Spiral, The Green Book, Tribune, Understanding, Verse, Wasafiri* (U.K.); *The Age, Fine Line, Luna, Meanjin, New Poetry, Northern Perspective, Overland, Southerly, Weekend Australian* (Australia); *Poetry Ireland* (Ireland); *Antipodes* (U.S.); and the anthologies, *A Time to Choose* (Backyard Press collection of Anti-Nuclear poetry, 1984, Melbourne), *Up From Below* (Redress Press collection of Australian women's poetry, 1987, Sydney), and *Kiwi and Emu* (Butterfly Books' collection of New Zealand and Australian women's poetry, 1989, Sydney).

Poems have been broadcast on the B.B.C.'s *Schools' Poetry Programme* (GCSE), on the A.B.C.'s *A First Hearing* and Radio 5UV (Adelaide).

Contents

Introduction

J ust as everybody likes tunes in music, so our taste, if we
admit to it, is for lyricism in poetry. The last two hundred
years have seen verse surrender to prose so much of the
public's attention — stories, comments, arguments, drama,
human character even: in return poetry has been given the
role of custodian of language and has become the place where
psychological understanding and the machinery of words
come together. This does not mean that poets today cannot
make poems out of the full range of experience which gets
into prose fiction and journalism. But it does suggest that
what they will be seeking is a distillation of the wider
world, a sense of packed feeling, of much contained in little,
and that the words chosen will make a memorable shape in
their own right.

Katherine Gallagher's poetry obeys just these precepts, in
that it is never otiose, does not harangue or burden its
reader with piles of confirming evidence. No nail is driven in
further than it need be. But these are its negative virtues.
The positive ones come from truth, firstly to the limbs of
language, and secondly to the emotions which words have
been summoned to support. We all write and read poetry to
project and recall heightened states of feeling, though, we
hope, not incoherent ones. Gallagher's poetry is full of
measured pain and well-timed pleasure. Everything is clear,
however; we are recognizably in the world of twentieth-
century immanence. Memory goes back to the pioneer days of
the nineteenth century in Australia, but life leans forward
to urban and family affairs in the post-nuclear decades.

In her 'Poem for the Executioners', Katherine Gallagher
finds a lyrical proverbialism for her sense of horror, and will
not let us forget that gibbets are not superannuated in many
parts of the modern world:

> *Slowly the air recoils*
> *on another unheard plea*
> *and light is locked upon*
> *a desolate, marked tree.*

That 'locked' is an expression of her lapidary interest. In the duo of haikus which give the book its title, we are confronted by these lines: 'This jellyfish beached,/grey unsmiling Medusa —/a woman cast off.' What appears, at first sight, self-pity comes to seem just the world's casual underlining of what happens. Even cruelty is viewed as part of the contamination of our communal living, as in 'Girl Teasing Cat with Mouse':

> *the moment of no return —*
> *all spinning out of control.*
> *And the girl knowing and not caring.*

The girl is in a seventeeth-century Italian painting, and the struggling mouse and the excited cat are everyday sights in the harshness of the painter's world, as also is war, which is the overt subject of the poem. Many poems in this collection partake of this emblematic quality — words are few but their consequences are many.

Katherine Gallagher writes about her ancestors, men and women who survived tough options in the hard years of the settlement of Australia. So her poems look back on children dead in their first months, on farmwork at harvest time, and on struggle and hardship for the later generations who left the country to find an easier life in the city. She takes on air flights (there is a thesis to be written on the alienating yet invigorating dislocation Australians feel after so many passages across twelve thousand miles via the stoical 747s, traversing what I have heard called 'the aluminium curtain' which separates Australia from Europe) — she considers the difference in seasonal expectations in the Northern and Southern hemispheres — above all, she finds words for the ecstasies, calamities and bewilderments of love.

Fish-Rings on Water is a book as much about feeling as about touching and seeing. It never loses sight of what goes on in the depths, below the surface tension of appearance. Considering the river, in 'Scene on the Loire', she sums up her own perception of reality:

a mind
completely at ease except
in one place where undercurrents
break, take over, where
no swimmer would be safe.

Peter Porter

'There the sky
is torn by the human gesture.
Even if it be the last city you love.
Even if it be the heart's last journey.'
      Andriana Ierodiaconou,
      Going to New York, after Cavafy.

I

International

I take my countries as they come,
fall in beside other travellers
lifting their lives like lightweight
suitcases carried under the heart
— no questions asked.

On this trail I stake my futures,
know that beginnings are old hat
to be recognized like the moon's stare.

I tell myself this is no fool's
paradise, floating on clouds. Here
I ape survival, sing my cagey repertoire
and occasionally see myself dancing
in a space where hemispheres meet.

Firstborn

Five hours since the cut,
they carry you in — a little grandee
dewy as a bud, black hair combed
perfumed eau de cologne.

I count your fingers,
eye your bunched fists, perfect skin.
A finished work — wrapped white,
your own person.

I missed your first cry —
now you are here separate, defined.
My stomach twists knives
as I try to hold you, skin against skin,

little voyager
in from your cloud.
Quickly I claim you
as I will again and again.

My mother

My mother, sixteen,
looks out of her photograph,
serene as I have mostly known her
circling calls of children —
lives she stepped in and out of

flaring doubts as to whether she
should have married a farmer.
'I was never cut out for farm-life',
she reminisces, still haunted by her weatherboard-
house, locked to its rainless earth
and parched sky.

The garden was an island-escape
she willed into flower,
saving bath-water, dish-water,
every drop teaching
the pricelessness of water.

Now she has a town-haven
trailed with flowers, hanging-baskets,
shrubs. She moves about its green,
pieced in my mind like a child's jigsaw
of a woman in a garden, quiet, hands unfussing —
her flowers surrounding, ablaze.

Getting the crop in

(i.m. J.G., 1899–1977)

Back from school, we'd find him,
dust on stubbly-whiskers,
finishing a round — his team
'best in the district' always.

He'd stake his life on them
and us. We hung in there
perched on the footboard,
a row of sparrows twittering

watching the toes dig furrows,
seed dropping into golden seams
that the harrows covered over.
We were swept along by 'Whoas'

'Gee-offs' and intermittently,
'In the name of God we start again.'
He was eating back a century
driving a straight line. Later

we'd help unharness the team,
feed them chaff as they milled
around the trough. Then home,
hardworking (we imagined) country kids.

A girl's head

(after the poem, 'A boy's head' by Miroslav Holub)

In it there is a dream
that was started
before she was born,

and there is a globe
with hemispheres
which shall be happy.

There is her own spacecraft,
a chosen dress
and pictures of her friends.

There are shining rings
and a maze of mirrors.

There is a diary
for surprise occasions.

There is a horse springing hooves
across the sky.

There is a sea that
tides and swells
and cannot be mapped.

There is untold hope
in that no equation exactly
fits a head.

My first angel

(i.m. S.G., May–August, 1940)

It was the day of the funeral:
'Kiss your little sister goodbye,
she's an angel now,' my father said
lifting us up to her one by one.

Ten weeks old, pale
in a white scrolled-box,
she simply looked asleep —
the sister-baby

I'd rocked and made laugh.
It was hard to believe
I had my own angel, so silent, still,
with no wings or a tinsel star.

Later, I understood much more
as we prayed to her for cousins
away at the war and for the bombs
and fighting to end.

She had been spared all that,
Mother would say.

First Communicants, Chartres

Mediaeval glass shapes half-darknesses.
Children take their places singing,
faces holding the light as in a painting.

I cup up pictures from childhood —
a white dress, gift prayer-book, my father's story:
Napoleon confessing First Communion his greatest day.

Memories shredded, gathering like a knot —
tying together what I've lost,
what I can't have back.

Eastville, 1939

That day Uncle Tom was a hero.
Mostly he was unpopular just for
living with us in the old family home —
taking up space, thinking it was his.

Occasionally he and Dad, bush-boxers,
had bloody fist-fights. But I worshipped him,
would tell my sister, 'Tom's my Dad,
Daddy's your Dad.' The grown-ups laughed.

That morning driving home from Mass
we were skylarking on the back seat —
the Dodge door swung . . . a strip of gravel
and yellow dust, my sister flew out.

Amidst the cries, Tom grabbed her
by one leg. They called it a miracle.

Nettie Palmer to Frank Wilmot
('Furnley Maurice')

'. . . we never said Nettie and Vance, we always said Nettie'n'
Vance sliding the three words into a single puff of breath . . .'
(Arthur Phillips, at a plaque-laying ceremony to honour the
Palmers, 25 July, 1985)

There are always the poems
  what sky-splitting poems I would write
    if only

Vance is
determined
is

The time and the leisure escape me
  still there is Vance's writing
    he has won prizes

taking on
the country
a landscape

My prizes have been for criticism
  When do I get time you ask
    after the chores and the children?

We are
'the Palmers'
or 'Nettie'n'Vance'

Vance is taking on the country
  says we are living in a state of barbarism
    and poetry not enough to change it

'Nettie'n'Vance'
you say it
almost one syllable

Its audience too small he says
  we must develop prose and the drama
    an Australian literary tradition

a way of seeing
Our lives
run together

But if only I had the time for writing
  for my poetry
    I would like the time and the leisure

My life-story
my own
but it will never be

to exploit the tiny talent I've got
  to be more than a *hausfrau*
    my poems   a circuit

told
except through
my daughters

Reviews in the *TLS* and the *Bulletin*
  I was encouraged
    that was years ago

Now the poetry has become
  merely a laugh   a distraction
    to entertain the children

and my letters
Still
there were poems

criticism praised
to be remembered
reminding

(Nettie Palmer, Australian critic, essayist and poet, b.1885, d.1964)

Cinquain

(for Julien)

Forty
when I had you,
your baby voice gave me
back my childhood. How I anchored
the days . . .

Relic

It graces the Women's Centre —
an abandoned pushchair, no canvas,
only the frame, four wheels
and a handlebar:
a sculpture for all weathers,
left in the front garden.

Maybe someone with a sense of humour
dumped it here, a reminder.
The baby is missing, long grown.
The mother has also gone
leaving only this shrill shell
once part of herself.

Pianist

The Grand is kept superbly —
felt covering the keys,
woodwork mirror-bright.

She lifts the lid,
dusts, doesn't touch the
ivory teeth —

hasn't played in years.
There was the moment
when the piano stopped.

She'd like to test her practice-
board, cut the silence —
her teacher's voice again

talking of chances,
how it's possible to get there
with study and a lucky break.

Music dams inside her
chords melt to fever, mazurkas
at her finger-tips,

cues like choices
like children. After the second,
she knew the walk across a dais

had passed her by. Still,
moments assail like her reflection
vivid on the piano-lid.

Gwen John's women

'People are like shadows to me, I am a shadow.' (Gwen John)

They are an army —
the last line of resistance, and resolute.
Don't be deluded by their passiveness:
women hatted, nursing cats, praying,
looking ahead, away, out of the frame . . .
Women unused to being centre-stage.

Ghosts

Sometimes she studies sepia-dark photographs
from the 1940s — her mother
and grandmother doing farm-chores.

Theirs was never the good life
but occasionally she envies them
their slow days.

Were they to catch her up,
she would feel their reproaches rising
over her, like steam on her dark glasses.

'A gold river reaches to where I walk,
recedes as I now swim towards a sun gaining
full heat near evening. *There are no seasons,*
it says; and then, *There are so many.'*
Diane Fahey, *Indian Summer.*

II

Farewell poem

It would be my first trip,
thousands of miles past a dread

of leaving — I saw Australia draped
Dali-style on a thread.

Your hand closed over mine:
'You won't regret it', you said

placing our friendship —
another journey circling my head.

September afternoon, Jubilee Lake

Cootamundra,
golden wattle
blaze in rings of light.

I watch my mother
watching
this scene,

she and my father
often brought us here.
Now

lakeside-gums
reach tall, taller
shadows embracing

cool. Reflections
summon her
like memories.

Would she take her years
back, knowing what
they've brought?

I pour our tea,
wait, listen
hang on her words:

I the wandering daughter
trace her steps,
store this sky.

Calcutta–London bus journey

'. . . Each shifting shape of light
soaks into me, soaks through.'
       Lisa Rees, *Body of Water*.

I watch, eyes speared with distance,
try to remember all this in its own
clarity — line growing into line
colours multiplied like days. How I yearn
to be still, forget I'm a tourist

as newness catapaults — country after country
ranged into likes and unlikes,
impressions — a vividness that haunts
that I hoard like an inheritance
alongside language-snippets floating on my tongue.

Plane-journey momentums

The danger of travelling is how
it takes you over, caught in
that today-dress you wear
not for frills but for comfort —
in the confines of an air-tunnel
marked by arrows on inflight-maps.

You read, pick up earphones,
settle to a book, tell yourself
that any disasters are swaying outside
this steady balloon
where you balance the day,
maybe humouring your child
who is flying for the first time.

So much for trying to forget
your innate strangeness to this absurd
transitory life you've taken on —
these dizzying heights, circuits of chat,
odd secrets laced with reserve
and everything blended for your newest
neighbour as though you'd been
living side by side for a lifetime.

Art class on Observatory Hill, Sydney

Here, the sea's bowl —
the harbour with still, white boats
and coloured flags — a Dufy carnival,
lines crisscrossing, the arch of the bridge
against roofs of scattered houses, shops.
It is afternoon, late summer —
how the promise of ships lies lazily
across the myriad bays
reaching as far as the eye can see.

The landscape-class, easels set up
have it all leisurely before them.
Their canvasses reflect this bluest of light
where the tutor's words float like gulls
wheeling in and out among Moreton Bay figs.

Party-line

We called her the *Bush Telegraph* —
she made news travel like fire
in those pre-electricity days.
She ran the local exchange,
had all the time she could want —
pigeon-holed down everyone's chat.

There was no stopping her.
At times a terse, 'There's
someone on the line' worked;
even then, she took an ungodly time
to put the receiver down.

If you were calling
your best love long-distance,
it could cost a fortune. No wonder
the Post Office employed her;
she made a mint for them
just hanging on — first to know

who'd had a baby, an accident,
who'd fallen off a horse
or been nicked for speeding,
who'd died or divorced.
She had it all, it had her:
a lifestyle ladling gossip

free-fall. She even
interrupted calls to correct
some point — a Dorothy Dix
manqué, a public minder,
carrying the district in her head.

Traveller, Sydney–Melbourne bus

He said he knew the world
through a postman's eyes—

'places I've seen on letters
and parcels from everywhere.

Communication, it all finally
comes to that,' he announced

moving about the bus, sometimes
chatting heart-to-heart.

There was his failed marriage
and a son back in Oregon —

this world-trip was a way
of starting out among friends

across the globe. He even made it
sound simple. Soon he'd be off to Europe —

so many sights before he hit
the States again. But Australia, sure

he loved it: the variety, the people,
the Barrier Reef, the Outback.

Finally it was the beauty . . .
'I can see beauty in anything.'

He laughed, 'I see beauty in a T-shirt
with a thousand flies on it.'

Near Keith, South Australia

I turn off the highway, follow signs
to a mud-brick cottage
tapestried with bearded grass, hollyhocks,
lavender, geraniums, pigface, sage.

My great-grandmother
who smoked a clay-pipe and bore eight children
lived like this, within bowed walls,
a track up to the door.

Today everything's locked, the single window
rations light. I peer in, picture a family
here in two rooms, children taking turns
to move closer to the fire —

throwing on logs to break the frost
while parents hungered for the promised
good year.

For a brother

I often visit your grave,
talking to you as I place
roses on your stone or pick tulips
and wild hyacinths from the grounds.

You never answer . . .
How else approach the unspeakable
except through these small gestures:
flowers, pauses at the graveside?

I see you driving your car
the moment before. You are smiling . . .
We were advised to remember you like that.
Reckless, abandoned that day

we huddled together scanning photographs,
your twenty years silenced —
imagining what you'd say
if you were to walk in.

January morning in Hornsey

The snow is melting underfoot,
air floats in close and still,
the glare turns brighter, incandescent.
These are the signs, soon the white canvas
will crack open revealing this street —
its discreet houses so briefly transformed.

As yet the white spectacle holds —
a bare stage, piercingly silent.
My footfalls enter the twitter
of birds — town-sparrows
flitting among spindly branches
that unbelievably hold their weight.

Haikus

I

Snow-melt, the sun coin
tumbles gently — found money
from a white sky purse.

II

Blue crocus hats flare,
resplendent in dozy sun.
Which one shall I wear?

Before spring, Woodside

Sun sends shock-waves
through the park:
beech and chestnut, half-lit
buds, swell,

leaning outwards
to that point in the sky's tilt
where heat can burn
into their core —

such change from
only two days back
as I step along
still muddy paths

earth-crust clinging
to my boots, and see the sun
suddenly lift itself clear
for a space of minutes.

This sun cracks my head
wide-open.

Heatwave

Three a.m. — twenty degrees,
the house becalmed on its jagged peninsula.
How this heatwave lulls and stupefies,
polishes silvery with sweat —

leaves me nostalgic for another hemisphere
as birds snip through half-light,
tearing open the brimming air.
Words, sleep blur — cancel each other.

Still, the day won't be held back,
contained by sleep or words . . .
I've been sitting here forever,
book on chapter four. If I'm lucky

I'll be discovered dozing. But no,
five-thirty now and the day gathering speed
as the first train clears the station
severing night from day.

Scene on the Loire

All around, a lit stillness.
The moon, placed without shadow
leans like a diva
smiling at her reflection
while almost carelessly

the river spreads — a mind
completely at ease except
in one place where undercurrents
break, take over, where
no swimmer would be safe.

To Joe: in memoriam

It is November again, Parc de Vincennes,
the trees perfect globes of gold —
paper-trees, leaves stuck in place.
The wind rustles them as we jog past.
Today we'll bring back a branch,
in a few days the leaves will fade.

When we run you say, 'Lift your feet
lift your feet,' encouraging me
as you encouraged me out of hopeless
love-affairs. I am running after you brother,
we are sifting gold in a hollow afternoon.

Blind woman

Sometimes I meet her in my skin
as she taps her white stick
on the day's four walls,
curling her way
through circles of black,
cajoling, taking me with her
to wait . . .

Pictures of Venice

On the Grand Canal,
Approaching Rialto Bridge

Surrender the arch
within an arch,
the eye's cool span.

Over the water's shift,
the patterns' layered
shine.

Suddenly a million ripples
unmade,
make me.

In St. Mark's Basilica

Marble and mosaic,
the blend transfixed
historic
homing a golden age —

tradition and detail
sculptured,
lit splendid
into prayer.

From St. Mark's Bay,
Towards the Arsenal

Searching
ancient kingdoms

the lion and the mariner
go out to sea together

and the mariner does not question
what the lion cannot answer

as oceans uncoil
terrible glass.

At Treporti, Mid-August

The boats come and go for Burano

and groups of tourists
gather into boats —

a certain pattern
like this, restless

leave for the islands
while the sea
hooks its sounds
to the ear's shell.

Homecoming

Picking out lights over Darwin,
too dark to see
but the pilot mentions it . . .

People stir, half-waking
as if instinctively
aware of land below

drawing us into its
sweep of colour.
Now an iridescent sunrise

somewhere over Alice,
dawn-changing colours
in a frenzy,

breath arching the win-
dows. Slowly land becomes
dun-squared, grey-green,

an antipodean patchwork:
this was the explorers'
wasteland and their trial —

Sturt's inland sea
still waiting
as the earth drums messages

and the plane drones
through powdery air.
My head tilts into

the storm of arriving —
past distances, faces
that I have assembled

among words, puzzles stretched to
new meanings over lost times
spaces I can't name, never could.

40

'But love is a harsh and pure honey.
The world is brought alive with us
So many times.'
Vincent Buckley, *Places*.

Eros on the Underground

He paces the platform,
pin-striped suit, hair parted
clean in the middle,
smooth: a good school look.
She arrives breathless,
brandishing brief-case.
His chiding her for being late
hides pure relief that she's here.

In the train, they grip hands
so tightly she winces. It's a game —
they swing from strength to strength.
Now she's holding, squeezing his hands,
their eyes meet, daring —
love cresting, delirious
no *vin ordinaire*, this wine to be . . .

First time

Being in love helped —
we could have been sewn together
by the night.

Afterwards we lay in warm grass
staring at an inky
quilt of stars.

Indifferent as usual,
the sky didn't melt
as I felt it might —

but still we wooed it,
peeled off our old skins —
gave heaven a twist.

Punk girl and friend

Her hair arrows out
    spiked like sun's rays
    in a child's drawing.

Her head is royal:
    is she flaring her way
    to some tribal fest?

He walks beside her, undiademed,
    dressed in suit and tie,
    hair slicked down

last night's punk
    taking on the face
    of the man from the office.

At any moment
    I expect them to declaim
    how they are night-birds

suddenly strayed
    into this morning's light
    that they must negotiate

through the eight-thirty rush.
    Briefly the street stops,
    all eyes focused as she moves

shooting sparks, edging him with tinsel
    and hand in hand
    they head south to the city.

The affair

He had a way of looking at the clock
when he arrived,

while undressing. She never
looked at the clock,

knew he'd leave
after an hour or two

and his fetish
was a way of letting her understand

he'd be home
as usual, for dinner.

Still, this was safe,
they could go on for years —

wait, phone-call, visit.
Not enough, but it was something.

How little, she realized one day
when he sent her flowers,

remembering her birth-
day and she cried.

Premonition

He splintered his songs —
they flew about, brittling the air.
She hovered, a moth in his way.

As he left early again, with excuses
she saw him freeze-framed —
silhouetted against her day.

Haikus

III

Fish-rings on water,
shining ribs under satin —
someone is breathing.

IV

This jellyfish beached,
grey unsmiling Medusa —
a woman cast off.

49

Alone on a beach

Alone on a beach
in the company of lovers

you watch the afternoon
lift steady as the waves

one especially insistent
hitting rock   changing colour

disappearing   then
coming again

a hot tongue licking stone

Reading Tsvetaeva

Love guiding her
like a candle-flame

Love tripping her
into step with herself

Love   the excuse for living
the ladder she would build and die on

Love   the blood-song
that began and ended with poetry

Love telling limits
borders she would choose recklessly

Fable

Writing from an eyrie in the Alps
you choose dried mountain flowers
to go with your texts.

No-one else has read them
and you say they're worthless . . .
I don't believe you.

Trust the tale not the teller —
an old adage, as the words stumble
like tired climbers

finding their way down at last.
You have breathed more life
into them than you know.

Lines for an ex

You used to say thousands of people
have died without water
but no-one ever died without love.

I got the gist — it hurt like hell.
I longed to prove you wrong
which you were, with your excuses.

Part of me still loves you though —
a shade . . . For love's sake,
I would go without water.

The good life

They are remarkable
for their parties, such *savoir-vivre*.
He has a group coming for dinner,
she is all he could want.

At a pinch, he can don an apron himself
while she cooks in several languages.
Their protean lives criss-cross
through food and friends.

Committed famously to good-housekeeping
they try out the right herbal messages,
put their whole lives in order.
The garden is for 'distinctive sharing' too —

their speciality on summer evenings
the terrace lined with a full neat lawn
of birds and voices. And flowers —
they pick bowls and bowls for the table.

Their lives are endlessly complete,
only sometimes in the distance
a child's voice startles.

Couple at a party

She glitters, laughs till her ribcage
strains — breath runs to metal.

He hears her bristling
against him, a whisper away.

When he interrupts her
the others pause.

She pretends nothing's
happened — freezes

crushes her love, brings the sky
down on their heads —

in this grief for a silence
without embraces or touch.

Old quarrel

Your face turns in a scowl
I guess at.
    I answer from my promontory
and trespass over lands we'd agreed to
leave alone.
    There's nothing new
you say, listing ghosts we always
bring up somehow.
    In the day's hard-edge,
intent's a mystery.
    Jab, push —
we can't leave it there, think we've found
the front-line.
    And our words
stare back at us — accusing, long-distance,
unsuccessful as bad photographs.

Flying

(for B.)

Remember, when you held my hand
over a restaurant-table
in the shadow of Notre Dame.
Already, my head was flying,
I wanted this wild happiness

to last. 'I'll have that hand',
you said, and we grinned at our beginnings
which were also endings —
the past without you seemed remote.
Here was the postscript

I'd been searching for
proving life could begin again
at thirty-five or forty
as we stormed landings,
scanned futures

felt love sitting lightly
on our shoulders, a cocoon
spun and spun, busy with
perfections — holding whole days
in its embrace.

'Every bone became a branch,
a bough, a twig. Inside her
the years settled in circles,
the spine hardened into heartwood.'

Helane Levine-Keating,
The Woman Who Lived in Trees.

IV

Waking, with variations

Waking up drunk
Waking up hungry
Waking up pregnant
Waking up to a birthday
Waking up beside yourself
Waking up with no time to lose
Waking up like Sleeping Beauty
Waking up to the Doomsday Clock
Waking up in another language
Waking up with a lover
Waking up to the system
Waking up to yourself
Waking up as a human
Waking up angry
Waking up numb
Waking up
Waking

Displacements

If the leaf-shadow
weren't there

there'd be grey path
without colour-shade

and if a girl weren't
walking over the leaf-shadow
there'd be path
and perhaps another walker

and if the path weren't there
there'd be earth
with leaf-shadow

and if the sun were to stay out
all the time
there'd be more leaf-shadow

and if the tree
weren't there

Conkers

We searched the park's waving grass,
sticks, wet bark, hunting conkers.
They lay half-hidden, waiting
to be discovered, shone again
in the neighbourliness of a child's pocket.

Gathered like prizes, they were:
deep-umber, singular, burnished, smooth,
there for the taking, curving each to each
their new wholeness. We combed that place.
Autumn nuggets — who would find the most?

Later some were threaded, hung loosely
on strings, to be taken to school.
Days after, they'd outlived their
first interest, mere leftovers
from a school-game — wrinkled,
shrunken to old copies of themselves.

Moon-talk

Moon, creamy white stone,
precious . . . Stick with the legends —
better at a distance.

My litany could go on —
I don't want to visit,
take a machine-ride against gravity

brain-open.
But if I change my mind
Moon won't have any say in it.

Third-year maths

Ribbons of chatter jostle boredom
as students cut into revision:
problems, percentages, while

grey walls show painted-charts
on enlargement, reflection, rotation —
pinpoint puzzles of seeing.

Maths is fun, they outrageously declare
as suddenly the pale sun
floats saffron bars across the desks.

The students look up, surprised, shake themselves
smile, hunch again over their work —
doggedly tracking the future's unknown,

balancing themselves against its *x*
as on the wall Escher's *Day and Night*
shows the birds flying into

light and dark — poised, always arriving,
all their chances imagined
still before them.

Untitled

Dearest Perce,
    I can understand your wanting to be a nurse,
but you're Daddy's and my only son —
you've always been our special one . . .

If you only knew how we've tried
to make your life an easy ride.
You never did like that school —
but what it cost! And who'll
be any wiser if you're just a nurse?

    My darling, I could curse —
the undertaking-business never worse.
All that stress on Dad, and now if you refuse
to drive the hearse, he'll lose
heart. The choice between lifting the dead
and the sick isn't easy — I dread
how either would take its toll
on a quiet, sensitive soul . . .

    Perce love, if you'd only phone. I'm so glum,
worried stiff. Sorry to moan,
               Mum.

Birthing

I burn
silvery through night.

Air wraps me, fills my pores.
I am lifted shell-like
into the day, past

the shift of voices, my voice —
a stranger naming milestones.

Wind settling my feet
within the rip
and slant of gravity.

Mood-stones

I

Catch a stone flung
or gems from shadows

Under an emptying sun
you hunt new colours

You are trying to portray
love as it is

II

Now turn to the stone
that shatters inside you

Colours fragmented
like glass

A link-up of splinters
and past filling present

Song

The cries of birds colour the earth
with song reaching clouds
of no destination.

The cries of birds warm the earth
lighting each continent
wakening sky.

The cries of birds deliver the earth,
entering your heart
promising nothing.

It is written

(for Shahnaz who told me the story)

She died in seconds
her chador catching fire
burning its envelope,
closing on her screams.

None of the men there
dared touch her
for under the law
only a husband
may touch his woman's body . . .

Their reason
for hesitating.

Poem for the executioners

This is a blinding-place.
Only the hangmen see
fixing the knot of shame
upon their chosen tree.

Moments of waiting shrill,
finally echo out
past the creak of startled wood
and a soon-muffled shout.

Slowly the air recoils
on another unheard plea
and light is locked upon
a desolate, marked tree.

Political prisoners

(for Nelson Mandela & Bram Fischer)

They call from behind
the wires.

It's still the same message
fenced-off

and their truth floats
upwards. You can see it,

a kite held high, suspended
where nothing particular

is happening.
But they keep holding it

before the eyes
of their jailers

and it sails all winds
in a tiny patch of sky.

After a news-item

(Australasian Express, 26/10/82)

It is reported that
tonnes of radioactive sand
may have been dumped
on building and recreation-sites
in south-east Queensland.

But no alarm please
the Director of Public Health insists
contaminated sand would not of itself
do anything other than increase
life-time exposure to radiation.

Those with children will be glad
the Health Minister is confident
that sandpits at two hundred
Brisbane nursery-schools are safe
and free from radioactivity.

Give us this day our daily bread.
Give us this day.

Faces

There is no such thing as a normal face, except for medical precision.

Our senses gather round the face.

There is the face of your lover. If you were choosing a face to fall in love with, you might have chosen differently.

The energy in the face is a turning-point.

The camera dramatises the face.

You might judge a person first by his or her face. In some countries, women's faces are hidden.

Anger surrenders the face.

The face is a record. Find it in a mirror.

Many faces together make a crowd — dancing, labyrinthine, pushing, still. These speak for the present.

The death-mask speaks across time.

Meeting Bessie Head in Adelaide, March 1984

(i.m. 1937–86)

Cautiously she gazed at us
through luminous-dark eyes —
the scrutiny of a writer.

The sky was cobalt
— an African sky, she laughed
standing there in bright florals
on an Adelaide street. Earlier
we'd heard her read to the Festival,
bring a whole village to life.

— I hardly ever leave Botswana,
my publishers arranged all this.
Then, like a postscript — I live in Botswana
and don't trouble anyone. That way,
I get on with my writing.

Get on with my writing . . . Her words
spun over our conversation —
reminders, warnings,
juxtaposing her private and public
faces, censorships she'd walked against
carrying her testament — its knotted
circle of words.

Newgate, Wales

The heavy cliffs lean
angled, quiescent,
brooding on giant elbows
as the haze lifts.

Dazzled, I
push away the thought
that in nuclear war, mountains
would rise against us.

Käthe Kollwitz — 'The Face of War'

'The exhibition must mean something, for all the works
were extracted from my life . . .'
                    (Käthe Kollwitz, in a letter, April 16, 1917)

I

Black paint grits under my nails.
Always death, his death
leaping ahead. My son, eighteen,
how I begged him not to go.
I do not know the squalor he died in,
I only know how grief without hope
is waste.

I make hundreds of pictures
without their bringing me
closer to him — it is as though
I have lost the gift
to put my life into the work.

I am caught at forty-nine
fraught forever by what I cannot change.

II

In every house, there is death —
we are mesmerised, submerged.

For two years I have tried
to draw the mother
who takes her dead child in her arms —
I seek my son as I might find *him*
in the work, but nothing comes.

Only the tumult of the search
has dragged me on
to that point where
language has changed,
where I have changed.
I feared his death too much.

Impromptu

The Sun headline was *Gotcha.*
Seventeen-year-olds acted out
a bare-bones play.

They envied those there —
the regulars who'd signed up
into the real thing.

It would all be finished
before they had a run
at the Argies, alas.

They buried the *Belgrano,*
sank it over and over
in their London classroom —

cheering, holding up their papers
to chants of *Gotcha*
and walked on waves, no surrender.

Girl teasing cat with mouse

(after the painting by Guiseppe Maria Crespi, 1665–1747)

Girl dangles mouse —
its body half-crouched
head turned away, eyes feverish
while the cat stretches
larger-than-life ready to spring.
Its jet-eyes glint, pacing the moment,
impatient with the game.

These are the ingredients of war:
predators, lust, the moment of no return —
all spinning out of control.
And the girl knowing and not caring.

Last afternoon

The wards whirred:
nurses peering in
my turn to keep watch —
feeling your child
now more than ever,
all our conversations
down to whispered assurances.

You gripped my hands,
you had come so far
at this hard pace.
I wanted to carry you away
as you had carried me Mother,
hearing you again
Always a new baby
never time to hold you . . .

Now the pain swallowing —
your voice still real
as in a telephone-call
twelve thousand miles away.
Wanting you Mother,
angry with you because
it wasn't your fault —
angry with myself
for not having said more often
how I loved you.

It would have been simple
a small thing to do,
yet suddenly important
with the lights going out
too quickly and me carrying you
on my shoulders this final time
such a long way in the dark.

Tree-planting

(for Julien)

Five-year-olds plant an oak,
press the roots firm, their gift.
Late-autumn cold chills, distracts
but they fight back
with cheers and hugs
down their conga-line.

They are making a pact
for all the trees of their lives —
chosen forests:
trees they will draw and colour,
fill with birds and flaring-golds
— that they will climb

stand under in the rain
and be hidden by,
that they will keep
to gird rainforests:
mantled, drenched in a lattice
of undergrowth and light.